small world

Tidy up!

Gwenyth Swain

ZERO TO TEN

To find out more about the pictures in this book, turn to page 22.
To find out more about sharing this book with children, turn to page 24.

First published in this edition in Great Britain by Zero To Ten Limited, part of the Evans Publishing Group, 2A Portman Mansions, Chiltern St, London W1U 6NR

Reprinted 2007

Published by arrangement with Carolrhoda Books, Inc., a division of Lerner Publishing Group, 241 First Avenue North, Minneapolis, MN 55401, U.S.A. Copyright © 2002 by Gwenyth Swain

A CIP catalogue record for this book is available from the British Library.

ISBN: 1–84089–493–8
13-digit ISBN (from 1 Jan 2007) 978 1 84089 493 6

The photographs in this book are used with the permission of: © Linda Phillips/Photo Researchers, Inc., front cover; © Paul A. Souders/CORBIS, back cover; © Trip/M. Fairman, p. 1; © Trip/A. Semashko, p. 3; © Liba Taylor/CORBIS, p. 4; © Richard Hutchings/Photo Researchers, Inc., p. 5; © Bill Bachman, p. 6; © Bachman/Photo Researchers, Inc., p. 7; © Peter Turnley/CORBIS, p. 8; © Trip/H. Rogers, p. 9; © Trip/P. Mercea, p. 10; © Mark E. Gibson/Visuals Unlimited, Inc., p. 11; © Laura Dwight/CORBIS, p. 12, 21; © M. Bryan Ginsberg, p. 13, 14; © Jeff Greenberg/Visuals Unlimited, Inc., p. 15; © Trip/J. Sweeney, p. 16; © Kevin R. Morris/CORBIS, p. 17; © M. Bryan Ginsberg, p. 18; © Ecoscene/CORBIS, p. 19; © K. Cavanagh/Photo Researchers, Inc., p. 20.

What do you do to make things tidy?

Do you clean-up after yourself?

Do you pitch in when others need help?

There are big messes, small messes
and messes in between.

And every single one of them needs
to be cleaned.

So fill a tub.

Soap, rinse and scrub.

Beat it or sweep it.

Shake it or rake it.

Fold your clothes.
Stack them in a pile.

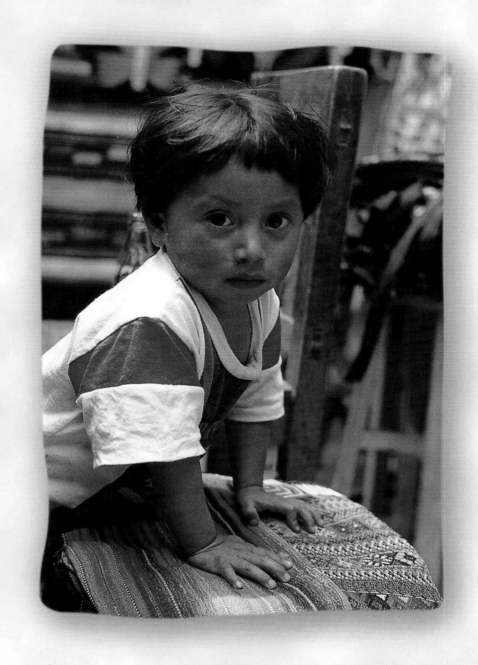

Make things neat.
You'll make others smile.

Do you need to do chores
before you can play?

Then shoo, shoo dust bunnies!
Get out of the way!

A mess looks like a mountain
until someone lends a hand.

So grab yourself a broom.
Help clean the grounds.

Straighten up.

Share the load.

Scrub it clean together.

Tidy up as you go!

More about the Pictures

Front cover: Asian American siblings tidy up their room.

Back cover and page 3: A boy in Moscow, Russia, takes out the rubbish.

Page 1: A young girl helps wash up in the kitchen, in Surrey, England.

Page 4: Even the youngest ones help clean up after a meal in Tanzania in East Africa.

Page 5: In the United States three children work together to wash their dog.

Page 6: Students carry out their annual roadside litter cleanup in the town of Thallon, in Queensland, Australia.

Page 7: This American eight-year-old boy will have a lot to clean up when he's finished his art project.

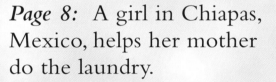

Page 8: A girl in Chiapas, Mexico, helps her mother do the laundry.

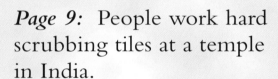

Page 9: People work hard scrubbing tiles at a temple in India.

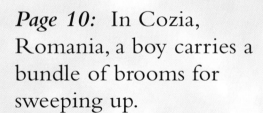

Page 10: In Cozia, Romania, a boy carries a bundle of brooms for sweeping up.

 *Page 11:* Children in California, USA, work together to rake autumn leaves.

 *Page 12:* Piles of clean laundry grow higher and higher as this boy helps his father in New York City, USA.

 *Page 13:* A boy in Guatemala tidies up by folding a blanket neatly.

 *Page 14:* In Sri Lanka, a girl collects water.

Page 15: Vacuuming is an important chore for this boy in New Jersey, USA.

Page 16: Children in Indonesia find that dishes get clean faster when you work together.

Page 17: In Thailand, boys sweep the temple grounds.

Page 18: A boy in Mexico helps tidy up near his home.

Page 19: School children in Britain line up to deposit their drink cans in a recycling bin.

Page 20: A father and son soap and scrub their car.

Page 21: This eleven-year-old girl tidies up by ironing her clothes.

A Note to Adults on Sharing This Book

Help your child become a lifelong reader. Read this book together, taking turns as you both read out loud. Look over the photographs and choose your favourites. Sound out new words and go back to them later to look at them again. Then try these 'extensions' – activities that extend the experience of reading and build discussion and problem-solving skills.

Talk about Cleaning

All around the world, people young and old work hard to keep things neat and tidy. Ask your child to describe the things he or she does to tidy up around the house, at school, or in the community. Next, study this book together. Which activities does your child do? Ask your child which chores he or she does every day, once a week, or never. If your child says never, ask if he or she wants to try doing the chore, either now or in the future.

Tidy Up Together

With your child, talk about the different things you do to tidy up. Choose one chore that you can do together at least once a week. Could your child help you to clean the car or wash the dishes? Discuss new ways you could tidy up together. How about taking a rubbish bag along the next time you and your child go for a walk, picking up rubbish as you go? Or how about offering to help a neighbour weed the garden or rake leaves?